Usborne Starting Point History

Who were the Romans?

Phil Roxbee Cox

Illustrated by Annabel Spenceley

Designed by Diane Thistlethwaite

Series editor: Jane Chisholm
History consultant: Dr Anne Millard

Additional illustrations by Kate Davies
With thanks to Andy Dixon

CONTENTS

Who were the Romans?

People who come from the city of Rome are called Romans. It was the same over two and a half thousand years ago. Rome is in the part of Europe now known as Italy. Over the years, the Romans took over many countries, making them part of a huge empire.

What are BC and AD?

These letters are used in dates. For example, 100BC means "100 years Before Christ". AD100 stands for "100 *Anno Domini* ", which is Latin for "in the year of our Lord 100". That's 100 years after the birth of Christ.

These citizens are very rich. They are called "patricians".

These purple lines show that these "patricians" are senators.

This is a "plebeian", an ordinary common citizen.

This woman has just bitten her "lingua".

These two citizens are called "equites". They are businessmen.

How many Romans were there?

Nobody actually counted them all but, when the empire was at its biggest, there were probably about 60 million people in it.

Who was in charge?

Rome was first ruled by kings, then by senators and finally by emperors. Certain people, called citizens, voted to choose which senators should have important jobs.

Who were citizens?

There were three types of citizens, and they were all men. You will find examples of each type on this page. Women and children could not vote.

2

What is Latin?

The language used by Ancient Romans. Latin is no longer spoken, except by people interested in learning it. Many words in many languages are based on Latin. In fact, the word "language" comes from the Latin word *lingua*, which means "tongue".

This woman is being carried in a special chair called a litter. This is nice for her, but not much fun for those carrying her.

Who founded Rome?

"Founded" means set up. Legend says that Rome was founded by twins named Romulus and Remus, in 753BC. As babies, they were abandoned and were brought up by a she-wolf.

Statue of the she-wolf

A man telling the tale of how Romulus later killed Remus and called the city after himself.

Slaves

How do we know what we know about Ancient Rome?

A lot of what we know comes from the work of archeologists. These are people who carefully dig up the remains of Ancient Roman buildings, and of Ancient Romans too. This kind of digging is called excavating.

Archeologist

Wine jars

Another archeologist

These archeologists are excavating a store where Romans could buy hot and cold drinks.

Serving counter

Many things written by Roman writers have also survived. This adds to our idea of life in Roman times.

Who and what were slaves?

Slaves were people owned by other people. They had to work hard and do horrible jobs for them. They didn't even get paid. Slaves usually came from the countries that the Romans had conquered. Some were treated very badly.

Who was Julius Caesar?

A popular general who ruled Rome, and made enemies too. On March 15 44BC, he was stabbed by a group of men. One of them was Brutus, who was supposed to be his friend!

A Roman dagger

3

What did they look like?

Early Romans came from a tribe called the Latins. Latins had olive skin and dark hair. When their empire spread across Europe, other people began to settle in Rome. As time went on, the Romans included people with lots of different looks.

This wall-painting shows us what one wealthy young Roman woman looked like.

What clothes did they wear?

Most Roman men wore tunics. If they were citizens, they could wear white robes, called togas, over them. Rich women also wore tunics, but wore bright dresses, instead of togas, on top. The Romans used to dye their clothes with different vegetable dyes.

Did they have different hairstyles?

Yes and, like today, fashions changed. Over the centuries, women's hairstyles became more and more spectacular.

A tunic

This man is wearing a toga because he is a citizen.

A "bulla", to keep away evil spirits

A simple dress called a "stolla"

A tunic under a "stolla"

Toga

This man has just had a beard trim. The mirror he is admiring himself in is made from polished metal, not glass.

Barber's assistant

Trimmed beard

Satisfied customer

Did they have shoes?

Yes, lots of different kinds. Women wore elegant sandals, but a soldier's boots were studded with nails. That way he didn't wear them out with all that marching.

Some Roman footwear

Soldier's boot

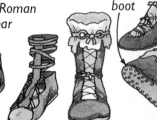

4

Did they wear make-up?

The women did. It was supposed to be beautiful to look very pale. This was probably to show that you were rich enough not to have to work outdoors.

What were their jewels like?

Fantastic! Rich women wore wonderful necklaces, earrings, bracelets and headbands made of gold, ivory and precious stones.

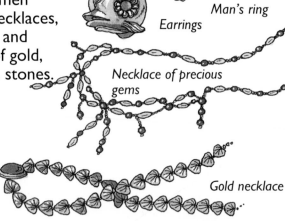

Earrings

Man's ring

Necklace of precious gems

Eyelids made darker using ash

Lips made redder with red wine

Face made paler with chalk powder

Gold bracelet

Gold necklace

Necklace

Perfume

A Roman table leg

Did they wear perfume?

Yes. Romans had many more baths and were a lot cleaner than people in other ancient civilizations. Both men and women loved wearing expensive perfume.

Did you know?

"A Roman nose" is still used to describe a particular type of nose that lots of Ancient Romans had.

A Roman

A Roman nose

How do you put on a toga?

Slowly! By studying statues and paintings, we think we know how it was done. You can make your own toga by carefully cutting up an old sheet. It won't be quite as big as the real thing.

Drape the left-hand end of the toga over your left shoulder.

Hold the other end in your right hand and bring it up under your arm.

Now throw the right end over your left shoulder.

Finally tuck the middle of your toga into your belt.

Tunic

Belt

A Roman boy's huge toga

1.10m (4ft 6in)

2.75m (9ft)

5

What were their houses like?

Rich people usually lived in a town house called a *domus*. Many of them also had a country house called a *villa*. But most people living in towns and cities rented an apartment called a *cenaculum*.

This is a typical villa.

Gardens

The family lives in this part.

What were their apartments like?

Some were very big and luxurious, but others had only one room. The poorest tenants lived on the top floors, which were often badly built out of old wood. These could catch fire easily and weren't very safe.

A Roman apartment building

Poor families live on this floor.

This floor has the nicest rooms.

A bakery

What was it like inside a Roman house?

The picture on the right will show you. Check the letters on the picture against those in the key box.

Key:
A The family bedrooms
B The kitchen
C The dining room, called the "triclinium"
D The "impluvium". A pool for catching rainwater
E The "atrium". The main meeting room in the house
F A guest room off the "atrium"
G A room rented out as a store
H The master's study

Did their houses have toilets?

Rich Romans' houses are thought to have had their own toilets. People in apartments probably shared public toilets in a room on the street level.

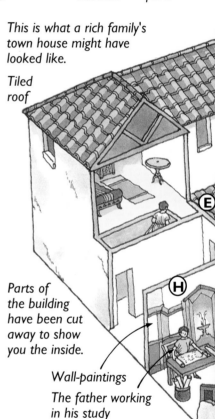

This is what a rich family's town house might have looked like.

Tiled roof

Parts of the building have been cut away to show you the inside.

Wall-paintings

The father working in his study

This Roman wall-painting looks like a view outside. The Romans didn't have wallpaper.

Did the Romans have electric light?

No, they usually used oil-burning lamps to light their homes. There were many different kinds of lamps. Three examples are shown on the right.

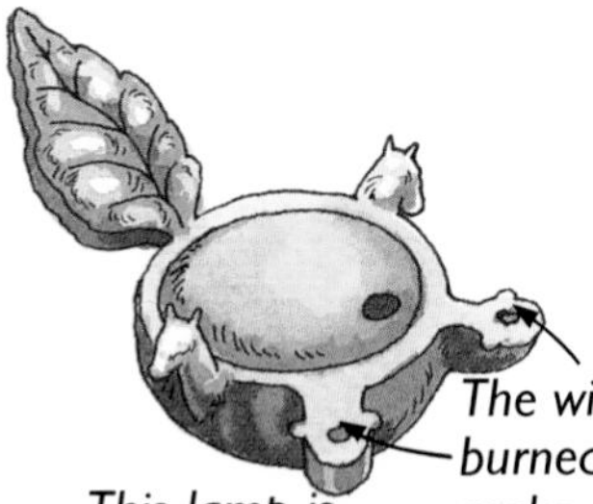

This lamp is made of pottery.

The wick is burned to make light.

Glass protects the flame.

This lantern is hung from the ceiling.

This stand, used to hang lamps on, is called a "candelabrum".

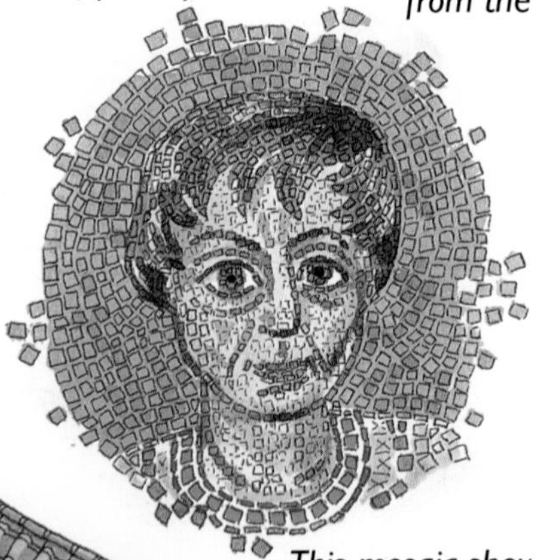

This mosaic shows a man's head.

Did they have carpets?

Romans might have used small rugs, but not carpets. Instead, expensive houses had patterned floors called mosaics, made from tiny pieces of stone.

How were mosaics made?

Smooth wet plaster was spread over the floor. Tiny squares of bright stone were pressed into it to make a picture. The gaps between the squares were then filled in with plaster.

How can I make my own mosaic?

One way is to cut pictures from a magazine into small pieces. Then stick them together, but leave gaps between the pieces. Here's another great way.

Cut cardboard into square pieces.

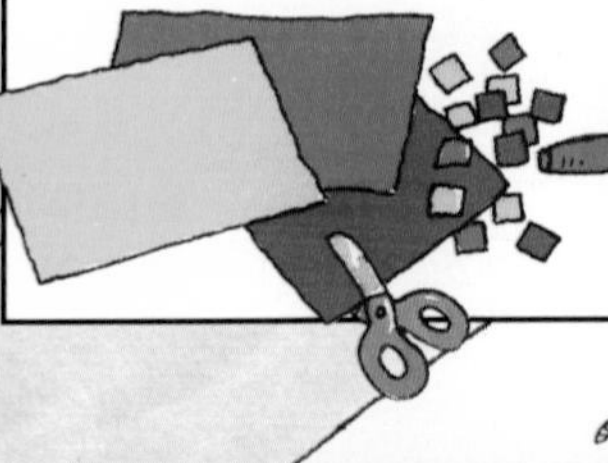

Roll out square of playdough.

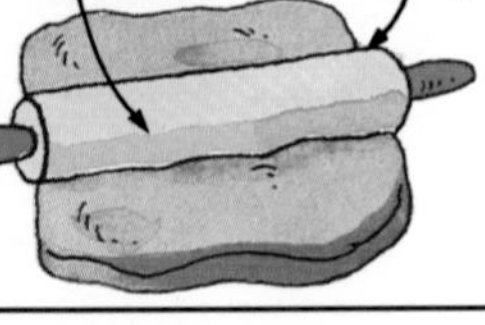

Rolling pin   Dough

Press the pieces of cardboard onto playdough base.

Mosaic pattern

7

There's more on the next page.

What furniture did Romans have?

All sorts. Most Roman furniture that is still around is made of marble or metal. That doesn't mean that they didn't have wooden furniture. It simply means that it has rotted away.

This Roman table is made of metal and wood.

A Roman stool like this was called a "scamnum".

What were their beds like?

Most beds were probably very plain and made from wood. Some beds, though, were very grand and used as couches in dining rooms.

This wicker chair with its high back is called a "cathedra".

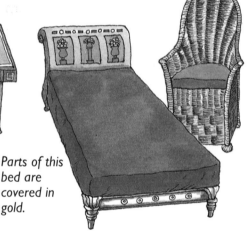

Parts of this bed are covered in gold.

Did the Romans have central heating?

Yes, they invented it. Roman central heating warmed rooms from under the floor. This was called a *hypocaust*.

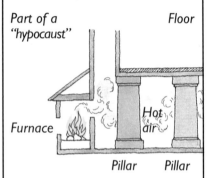

Part of a "hypocaust" *Floor*

Furnace *Hot air*

Pillar *Pillar*

How did they turn it up or down?

Archeologists can only guess the answer to this. Perhaps the temperature couldn't be changed. No one knows for sure.

Some "hypocausts" used pipes like these.

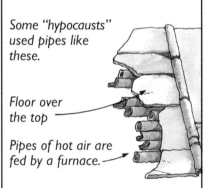

Floor over the top

Pipes of hot air are fed by a furnace.

How do you think they might have been able to change the temperature?

What were their kitchens like?

Apartments didn't have kitchens, so tenants had to buy ready-cooked food. Private houses, however, had large kitchens with different fires for cooking different types of food.

Pot of vegetables

Spit

This fire is being used to roast meat on a spit. A slave will have to turn the spit handle.

This fire is used for cooking vegetables on the top.

8

Where did they go shopping?

In large towns there were lots of different stores. Most of them didn't have doors or windows, but opened onto the street. The counters went right across the front of the stores, and the storekeepers stood behind them.

Stores were usually on the bottom floor of apartment buildings like these.

This man is buying furniture.

A weaver sells some cloth.

Menu

This man has drunk too much hot spiced wine.

A mistress, her shopping and her slave

A "plebeian" carrying his own shopping

People enjoying some stew

Who went shopping?

Rich Romans would only go shopping when they wanted to choose expensive things for themselves. Many of the richer Romans had paid servants. If they wanted ordinary things like food, they sent the servants, or slaves, instead.

Did they have supermarkets?

No. Although the Romans put up many large buildings, they didn't think of building supermarkets. Stores were usually very small. Those storekeepers who sold luxuries could make a lot of money.

This picture shows a Roman street corner, with people out shopping.

Did they have cafés?

Yes, there were places to buy hot food and drinks. Customers could eat the food there or take it with them.

9

There's more on the next page.

Did they have pharmacists?

Yes, but they weren't anything like the ones we know today. They sold magic spells as well as their special herbs and potions.

Did the Romans have outdoor markets?

Yes they did. As well as the usual stores, a town would also have market stalls. These were set up in the middle of town in a square called a *forum*. Markets were held once a week.

An outdoor Roman market in a town square

This shopper suspects that some meat has gone bad.

A thief stealing fruit

A fishmonger

His fish

A Roman dog shopping for scraps

Were there ever traffic jams?

Believe it or not, the answer is yes. In the city of Rome itself, there were hundreds of stores and houses needing goods. These had to be delivered in carts, and the roads often became blocked. Later, to stop this, horse-drawn carts and chariots were not allowed into the city during the day.

This stallholder is bringing his casks of wine to market very early in the morning.

Did you know they had special "toga cleaners"?

Men, called fullers, used to bleach the togas.

Frame

Toga

The togas were then put in a mixture of water and a special kind of clay.

Fullers tread on togas to get the dirt out.

Clay and water

Once the togas had dried, they were folded and pressed flat in a machine.

Flattened togas

Awnings keep the sun off food to keep it fresh.

This slave is filling his master's jug with wine.

A baker's stall

A fruit seller's stall

Auctioneer

Slaves

Bidders

A slave auction

Did they recycle packaging?

No, because nearly everything bought from a Roman store was loose. All bread, meat, and clothing would be sold unwrapped. There was no packaging, so it didn't need recycling.

Wine jars　　　　*Slaves*　　　*Mistress*

These shoppers don't have cars or plastic shopping bags.

If you were buying wine, you would take along your own jugs to be filled, or would buy a whole jar. This meant that no bottles needed to be recycled.

Where did Romans buy their slaves?

From a slave market, of course! The slaves would often wear signs around their necks saying what they were good at. They were sold by auction to the person who offered to pay the most.

What did people pay with?

The Romans had coins made from bronze, silver and gold. The gold ones were worth the most. Over the centuries, hundreds of different kinds of Roman coins have been found.

These coins are from different periods in Roman history.

The first kind of Roman coin. It was made of copper.

An "aes grave". The first type of round coin.

Silver coins, like this "denarius", were first used in about 200BC.

This coin was made to record the death of Julius Caesar.

Did Roman children go to school?

In the early days, rich Roman families paid private tutors to teach their children at home. Later, boys' schools were set up, but parents still had to pay to send their boys to them. This meant that poorer children never went to school, so they never learned to read or write. Very few girls were sent to school. Some were taught by their mothers.

What were the schools like?

Most schools had only one room and only one class. There were about twelve pupils. Schools were often above or behind a store.

This school is called a "ludus". It is for six to eleven year old boys.

This teacher is Greek. Many teachers were from Greece.

A bored boy

A scroll

This is a "paedagogus". He has been sent by this boy's parents to make sure he works hard.

This boy is writing a poem. By the look on his face, he probably thinks that it's pretty good.

This boy writes by scratching onto pieces of broken pottery.

Stylus

Wax tablet

What did they write on?

Not paper. The Romans did have a kind of paper made from reeds, and wrote on animal skins, but this was too expensive for children to write on. Schoolboys would usually write on wax tablets with a pointed stick called a stylus. They could then rub the wax smooth and start again.

12

Did they read books?

Yes. A school would have had a few books, but not like this one you are reading now. Printing had not been invented, so books had to be written by hand. They were usually made from one long piece of paper rolled around a stick. This was called a scroll. Later, a new type of book called a codex was invented. A codex was shaped more like a book today.

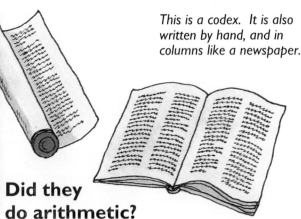

This is a scroll. It is 10m (over 30ft) long. The writing is in columns.

This is a codex. It is also written by hand, and in columns like a newspaper.

Did they do arithmetic?

Yes, and they didn't have electronic calculators. Roman numbers looked different from ours. They were written as capital letters. The Roman numbers from one to twelve are shown below.

This is an abacus. People slide the wooden balls along the wires as they count.

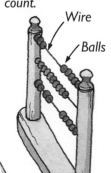

Wire

Balls

What else did they learn at school?

As well as reading, writing and numbers, boys were also expected to learn Greek. When they were older, boys could learn to speak in public if they wanted to be a politician or a lawyer. This could take years and was very expensive.

This boy is learning public speaking with a special teacher called a "rhetor".

What did the girls learn at home?

Girls in the richer Roman families were taught how to read and write, and run a household. Some of them had private tutors and music teachers.

This girl is being taught to play the lyre. It is made from a tortoise shell.

Lyre

A very old music teacher

What's the difference?

Roman numbers are still used for some things today. See if you can find a watch or clock with Roman numbers on its face. What is the difference between the Roman numbers on the clock and the more traditional Roman numbers shown on the left?

What did they do if they were ill?

They felt terrible! Many sick Romans slept in shrines built for Aesculapius, the god of medicine. They believed that the dreams they had in the shrines would tell them how to get better. Most people, however, went to see their doctors.

Did they have hospitals?

Yes, for very sick people. Rich Romans could pay more and have their doctors treat them at home. Very rich Romans had personal doctors. These doctors were paid to look after them and no one else.

A man learning to be a doctor

An army doctor

This soldier has hurt his leg in battle.

These men are inside an army hospital. It is in a tent near the battlefield.

Wine to help ease pain

Pill box

Blanket

Stick of ointment

Herbs for medicine

This lamp is used to light the tent after dark.

FIL·MEDICA

This carving on a tombstone shows a woman doctor.

How could you become a doctor?

People learned to be doctors in either army hospitals or medical schools. Most doctors were men. Historians think that women doctors had the special job of looking after women having babies. Having a baby was very dangerous in Roman times.

What if you couldn't pay for a doctor?

Some doctors did not have to pay taxes. This saved them money, so they treated their very poor patients for nothing.

14

Were they good at operations?

Yes. Roman doctors carried out some very serious operations. Many of these were successful. They included mending broken bones and cutting off limbs. Cutting off an arm or leg was easy. Making sure that the patient lived afterwards was the hard part!

This soldier has had his bad leg cut off.

Did they have medicine?

Yes. In fact, an army doctor called Discorides tested 600 herbs and 1000 drugs on his patients. He kept written records of which drugs he used for what. These lists still survive today.

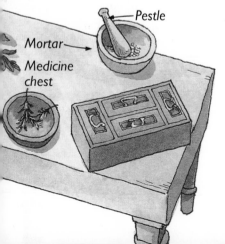

Pestle

Mortar

Medicine chest

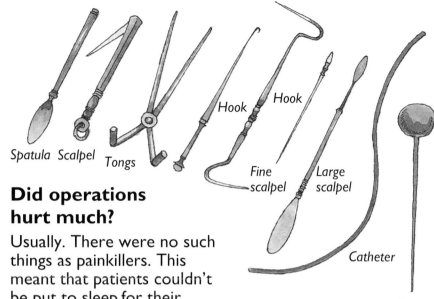

Spatula Scalpel Tongs Hook Hook Fine scalpel Large scalpel Catheter Spoon

These are just some of the Roman surgical implements (tools used in operations) that archeologists have discovered. No one knows exactly what they were all used for.

Did operations hurt much?

Usually. There were no such things as painkillers. This meant that patients couldn't be put to sleep for their operations. Sometimes patients were given alcohol to drink, but they would be awake and felt the pain. It can't have been much fun.

What do old bones tell us?

Archeologists have learned a lot about the skill of Roman doctors by studying skeletons.

Holes

A Roman's skull

The holes in this skull must have been made by a skilled doctor. He was probably trying to cure his patient of very bad headaches. Many people lived after this type of surgery.

What do you think this is?

The object shown below was made for a Roman patient to wear. It is shown actual size. (That means that it hasn't been drawn smaller to fit on the page.) What do you think it was used for?

CLUE: The metal parts, including the two screws, are made of gold so that they will not rust. The answer is on page 32.

15

What did Romans do for fun?

Romans had lots of different pastimes to keep them busy. There were simple games to play at home, plays to go to see and huge public events for thousands of people to watch. Because television and radio hadn't been invented, people actually went to the events themselves.

What games did children play?

Roman children had seesaws, swings, kites, hoops and toy houses to play with. *Tali* (knucklebones) was a game that was popular with grown-ups too. It was like rolling dice.

These knucklebones were used like dice.

This is an early version of draughts or checkers.

Did children have teddy bears?

No. Teddy bears were not invented until the 20th century, but there were wooden dolls.

This doll has joints in its arms and legs. The girl has taken off its clothes.

Which games did they like best?

The two games that Romans liked to watch the most were chariot racing and gladiator fights. Chariot races were the most popular of all sports. Sometimes there were twenty-four races a day.

This is a race track called the "Circus Maximus".

What were chariots?

A racing chariot was a small two-wheeled cart, pulled by fast horses. Racing was dangerous, and riders often fell off and were killed.

A brave driver

A racing chariot

16

Who and what were gladiators?

Gladiators were slaves or prisoners made to fight each other, or wild animals, in front of crowds. These fights were part of events called 'the games'. They took place in huge open-air buildings called amphitheatres. Successful gladiators were sometimes freed.

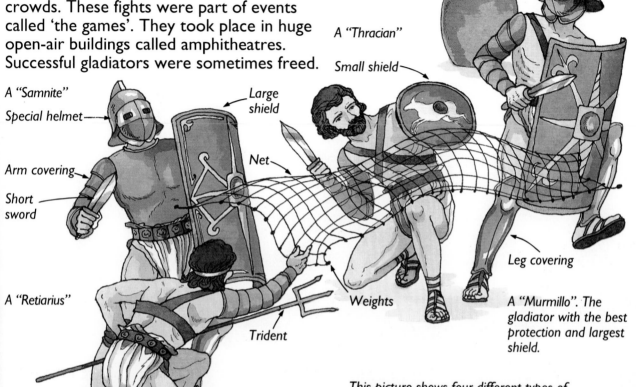

Helmet

A "Thracian"

Small shield

A "Samnite"

Special helmet

Large shield

Arm covering

Net

Short sword

A "Retiarius"

Trident

Weights

Leg covering

A "Murmillo". The gladiator with the best protection and largest shield.

This picture shows four different types of gladiator training together before a real fight. There is a "Samnite", a "Retarius", a "Thracian" and a "Murmillo". Each type uses different kinds of weapon and clothes for protection.

Did you know?

At the end of a gladiator fight, the emperor would often give a "thumbs up" or a "thumbs down" signal. This was to show whether he wanted the loser to live or to die.

An emperor

An emperor's thumb

We think that "thumbs up" meant "live". This is probably why the sign is still used today to mean that something is good, or is going well.

There's more on the next page.

What were theatres like?

In the early days of Rome, they were made of wood. Later, they were much bigger and built of stone. In the older ones, people had to stand up to watch the plays. This must have made their legs very tired. Later, stone seats (like steps) were built.

What were the plays about?

Early Roman plays were copied from Greek ones. There were two types: tragedies and comedies. A tragedy was a play with a sad ending. A comedy wasn't always a play full of jokes, but one with a happy ending. The Romans did like jokes, though.

These "women" are men dressed up. All actors were men.

This mosaic shows a scene from a play.

Romans watching a play

These people paid the most money so get the best view of the stage.

The stage was called the "pulpitum".

Poor people sit at the back.

These are all entrances and exits.

The seats are hard to sit on.

These poles can be used to hold up a canvas roof that keeps the sun off.

Could they buy snacks?

Yes. At big public events, there were usually people selling different kinds of food. Snacks were often fruit or vegetables. Romans wouldn't have been able to buy popcorn or ice cream.

This marble carving, called a relief, shows two actors in a play. They are both wearing masks.

Why did the actors wear masks?

Many Roman plays used the same characters, such as "the smiling fool" and "the wise old man". The actors wore masks so that it was easy to tell who they were playing from a distance. It must have been difficult to see much from the seats at the back anyway.

Did they have parties?

Yes. The Romans loved a good party. They often had them on public holidays, and there were plenty of those in Roman times.

Relaxing slaves

Their master

After "Saturnalia", the festival of the god Saturn, masters and mistresses actually held parties for their slaves!

What food did they eat?

At parties, rich Romans would have enormous feasts. They ate salads, eggs and shellfish for their first course. This was followed by a main course of up to seven dishes.

A slave serves some wine.

This scene shows a Roman dinner party.

People sit on couches.

A "cithara". A type of lyre.

The cymbals being played here were called "cymbala".

This is a Roman trumpet.

This man is playing a set of double pipes called "tibiae".

Did they listen to music?

Yes. They didn't have CDs, records, cassette tapes or radios. People went to concerts and heard music in the street and in the homes of rich citizens. There were many types of musical instruments.

This lyre is made out of wood and metal. Some were made from tortoise shells like the one in the party scene.

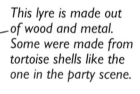

This is a "sistrum". The musician shakes it like a rattle.

Do we know what Roman music sounded like?

In a way. Archeologists have worked out what some Roman instruments probably sounded like. How do you think they managed to do that?

19

Did they have swimming pools?

Yes, they had them in buildings called bathhouses. These were much more than indoor swimming pools. They were fantastic places where a Roman could swim, bathe, take a sauna, have a massage, wrestle or just relax. Some bathhouses even had libraries attached to them. They were also used by Roman businessmen to hold meetings, or for friends to get together in.

Who could use the baths?

The public bathhouses were open to men and women, but they couldn't use them at the same time. The evenings were often for women only.

This is what a Roman bathhouse might have looked like. Parts of the roof, walls and floor have been left out so that you can see inside.

Did you have to pay to get in?

Yes, but the entrance fee was very cheap. In the days of the emperors, it cost only one *quadrans*. That was the smallest Roman coin there was.

What were the bathhouses like?

Amazing. They used very complicated heating systems to keep different baths and pools at different temperatures. People would go from one bath to another. The bigger bathhouses were usually beautifully decorated places.

This is the hottest bath in the house.

A very sweaty man

This businessman is enjoying a massage.

Underfloor heating system

How many were there?

By AD284, there were over a thousand private and public bathhouses spread across the empire. Hundreds of thousands of Romans must have spent many hours enjoying themselves in them.

Changing rooms

Did they have swimming lessons?

It is unlikely that bathhouses held official classes to teach people to swim. Most of the indoor pools were designed for people to bathe in. They were too small for swimming around in. People may have taught their friends in the bigger, outdoor pools.

Not with soap. To get rid of all the sweat and grime of everyday Roman living, they covered themselves with oil.

This Roman pot is full of oil.

Then they would scrape off the oil with special scrapers made of metal, wood or bone. These were called strigils. Some people had their slaves do the scraping for them.

These strigils are on a hoop so that they can be easily carried.

People actually live in these apartments. It's very noisy.

Wrestlers

No one is wearing a swimming suit.

Did the Romans keep animals?

Yes. Animals were an important part of Roman life. You will find them throughout this book. They were hunted, collected, and kept as pets. They carried goods and people, and pulled carts and equipment. The most popular pets were cats and dogs. Dogs were also used to guard houses.

This Roman mosaic is over 2,000 years old. The words are Latin for BEWARE OF THE DOG.

Did the Romans have zoos?

No. There were no zoos as we know them today. Wild animals were sometimes caught to be used in the games. The more unusual animals were simply shown to the crowds. Common animals, such as bears and bulls, were forced to fight each other or gladiators.

This picture, taken from part of a mosaic, shows an African elephant being ridden in the games.

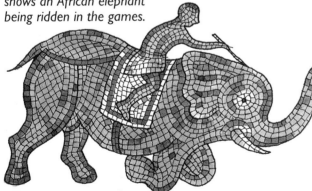

Why did the Romans go hunting?

This hunting scene is taken from a mosaic.

They trapped animals to take back alive for the games, and hunted more common animals to eat. They went fishing too. The picture above shows hunters capturing a wild boar, which is a kind of hairy pig.

This is taken from a Roman painting. The Roman artist did not draw to scale.

African animals

Were people really thrown to the lions?

Yes. They were usually people who were thought of as criminals. These included Christians and Jews who refused to worship Roman gods. During the games, they would be thrown to wild animals to die.

What farm animals did they keep?

The Romans kept animals to use for food, such as chickens, pigeons, pigs and sheep. They also kept working animals such as cattle, horses, donkeys, camels and dogs.

Goats were very popular because their milk made tasty cheese. Sheep were kept for their wool and for milk too. The Romans really liked sheep's milk.

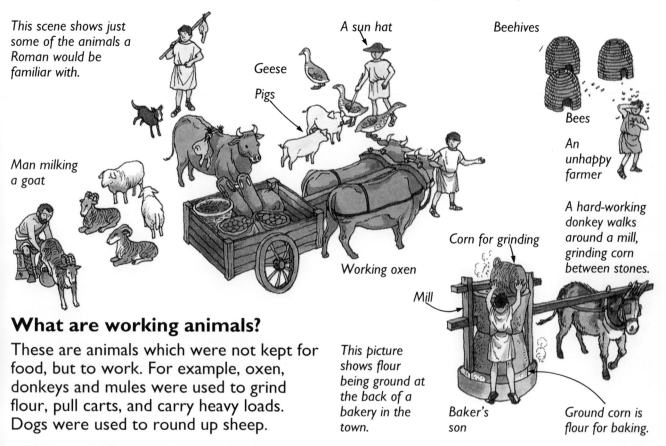

This scene shows just some of the animals a Roman would be familiar with.

Geese

Pigs

A sun hat

Beehives

Bees

An unhappy farmer

Man milking a goat

A hard-working donkey walks around a mill, grinding corn between stones.

Corn for grinding

Working oxen

Mill

What are working animals?

These are animals which were not kept for food, but to work. For example, oxen, donkeys and mules were used to grind flour, pull carts, and carry heavy loads. Dogs were used to round up sheep.

This picture shows flour being ground at the back of a bakery in the town.

Baker's son

Ground corn is flour for baking.

Did you know?

The Roman Emperor Gaius (who was nicknamed Caligula) tried to make his horse a consul. This was strange, because a consul was the most important job in the government!

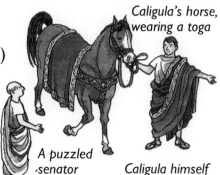

Caligula's horse, wearing a toga

A puzzled senator

Caligula himself

Caligula got his name from the Latin word for the small soldier's boots (*caligae*) he used to wear. After a few months as emperor, he became sick and is thought to have gone mad.

Did the Romans believe in God?

By the time the Roman Empire came to an end, Rome's official religion was Christianity. Throughout most of Rome's long history, however, most people believed in many different gods, goddesses and spirits. Each of these had special duties.

Where did their gods come from?

As well as their own gods, Romans often worshipped gods from the countries they invaded. They gave these gods Roman names. Many Roman gods were first worshipped in Greece.

Each house had a little altar like this one, called a "lararium".

This family is praying to house spirits.

Who or what were the spirits?

Less important Roman gods. Each family had its own spirit, called a *genius*, to guard it. Different parts of a house were protected by different spirits. For example, Janus **24** was the spirit of doorways.

This is what many Roman temples looked like. They were based on Greek ones.

Did Romans go to church?

They went to temples or shrines dedicated to particular gods or goddesses. These were looked after by priests and priestesses, who were very important people. Many temples were full of beautiful treasures.

Did they believe in heaven?

Yes. People thought that a dead person's spirit was rowed across the River Styx to an underworld, called Hades.

Hades

The entrance to Hades is guarded by a dog with three heads.

River Styx

Here the spirit was judged and either sent to heaven (*Elysium*) or hell (*Tartarus*).

What did their gods look like?

People believed that their gods looked and dressed like them. Some gods were thought to be enormous and able to turn into animals and objects.

This picture shows the god Jupiter disguised as a bull.

What duties did the gods have?

Each god was in charge of a certain area of life. For example, Ceres was the goddess of crops. Roman farmers used to pray to her for a good harvest.

On this page and the next one, you will find pictures of some important Roman gods. Their Greek names are written next to their Roman ones.

Jupiter (Zeus).
King of the gods and god of thunder and lightning.

Juno (Hera).
Goddess of women and childbirth.

Mercury (Hermes).
Jupiter's messenger and god of trade and thieves.

Minerva (Athena).
Goddess of wisdom, crafts and war.

Bacchus (Dionysus)
God of wine.

Did you know?

The goddess Vesta had a very special shrine in the middle of Rome. Inside it, a fire burned all the time. Many people believed that if the flames went out, the Roman Empire would collapse. The fire and the shrine were looked after by a group of six women.

They were called the Vestal Virgins. It was very special to be chosen to be one of the six. A Vestal Virgin could not marry for the thirty years that she had to look after the sacred fire.

This is a carving of the Vestal Virgins dressed in their robes.

There's more on the next page.

What did the gods do all day?

Although they had special powers, they often behaved like ordinary people. They argued, got jealous and even tried to trick each other.

There is a famous story about Roman gods and goddesses on the next page, and more pictures of them below.

Diana (Artemis). Goddess of hunting and the moon.

Neptune (Poseidon). God of the sea.

Venus (Aphrodite). Goddess of love and beauty.

Did they sacrifice animals?

This animal is about to be sacrificed to Mars, the god of war.

Yes. Animals were often killed and given as gifts to particular Roman gods. Animals were also used by religious fortune tellers. By looking at the insides of a sacrificed animal, some Roman priests believed that they could see into the future.

Who were these gods and goddesses?

Here are images of three Roman gods or goddesses. They are taken from a carving, a statue and a wall-painting. By looking at their clothes and what they are holding, archeologists can tell who they are supposed to be. Can you?

A carving

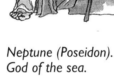

A marble statue

Part of a wall-painting

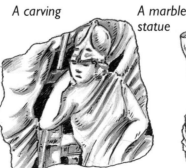

The sad goddess and the seasons.

Long long ago, when the gods still walked upon the Earth, Ceres, the goddess of crops and harvests, had a daughter. Her name was Proserpina and she was dazzlingly beautiful.

One day Dis, the god of the Underworld, saw Proserpina and instantly fell in love with her. He knew that she would not choose to live with him in his gloomy world of the dead, so he seized her, and took her to the Underworld in his chariot.

Ceres hunted high and low for her missing daughter. Nothing else mattered to her. She left the plants and crops to die so people began to starve. When she found out what Dis had done, she pleaded with Jupiter, king of the gods, to return Proserpina to her.

Jupiter agreed, so long as Proserpina hadn't eaten the food of the dead while living in the Underworld. In fact, Proserpina had been so sad that she hadn't eaten a single thing . . . until Dis tricked her into tasting six pomegranate seeds, so that she would have to stay with him forever.

Jupiter was furious that Dis had deliberately tricked Proserpina, so he allowed her to go back to her mother. This was on the condition that she returned to Dis for six months of every year. That was one month for each of the pomegranate seeds she had eaten.

Whenever Proserpina was released, her mother was happy and the crops and plants began to grow. This became known as spring and summer time. Whenever Proserpina had to return to the Underworld, her mother became sad again and leaves fell from the trees and later died. This was autumn and winter. And that is how we come to have different seasons.

What was the Roman army like?

Very big and very well organized. One reason why the Romans had such a large empire was because they had such a strong army to fight for it. At one time, there were as many as 450,000 soldiers.

Who could be a soldier?

Land-owning men between 17 and 45 could be forced to become soldiers for a while. By 100BC, most soldiers were full-time. They stayed in the army for 20 to 25 years.

How was the army organized?

In small groups, big groups and enormous groups. A group of eight soldiers was called a *contubernium*. Eight of these made up a group called a century. Centuries were grouped into cohorts, and eight cohorts made up a legion.

These ordinary foot soldiers have just finished a day's march.

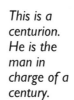

This is a centurion. He is the man in charge of a century.

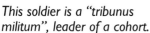

This soldier is a "tribunus militum", leader of a cohort.

Battle orders

This is a "legatus". He is leader of a legion.

An army horse

What were their army camps like?

There were two kinds of camp. One was made up of tents, which could be taken down and moved quickly. The other was built of stone.

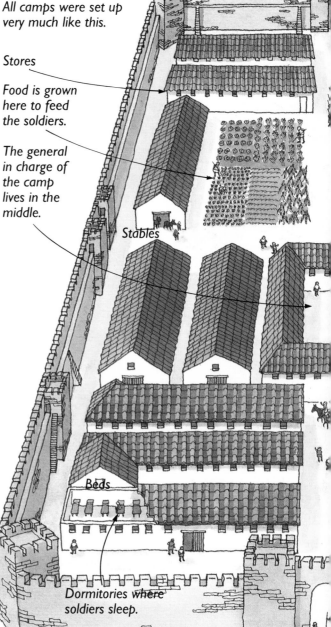

All camps were set up very much like this.

Stores

Food is grown here to feed the soldiers.

The general in charge of the camp lives in the middle.

Stables

Beds

Dormitories where soldiers sleep.

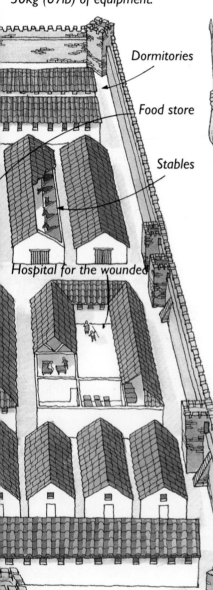

The soldiers in the camp are training. They have to march all day while carrying 30kg (67lb) of equipment.

Dormitories

Food store

Stables

Hospital for the wounded

Lookout tower

What uniforms did they wear?

Different types of soldier wore different uniforms. Here are two examples:

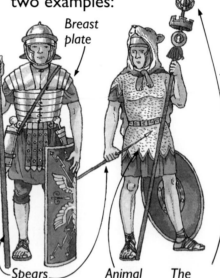

Breast plate

Spears

Animal skin

The standard

The soldier on the left is a legionary. The other man is a standard bearer. Each legion had its own standard with an eagle on top.

Did they have guns?

No, but they had lots of weapons, big and small. The smallest was a dagger. The largest were siege towers, battering rams and catapults.

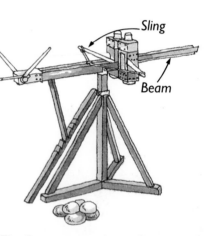

Sling

Beam

This Roman catapult can fire stones up to 30m (92ft).

A siege tower was a wooden tower on wheels. Soldiers could dash out of the tower onto the top of the walls of enemy forts.

Did you know?

In battle, Roman soldiers sometimes grouped together and held their shields all around them. They called this "the tortoise". The soldiers protected themselves in the same way a tortoise does with its shell.

A typical army tortoise

Did the Romans only build buildings?

No. As well as putting up apartment buildings, villas, stores, temples, bathhouses and lots of other types of buildings, Romans are famous for building aqueducts and roads.

This picture shows what an enormous Roman building site might have looked like. An aqueduct and a road are both being built.

What was an aqueduct?

An aqueduct was a pipe or channel that carried water from a well or stream to towns and cities. Some aqueducts were buried underground. The more famous Roman aqueducts were like huge bridges carrying the water along the top. *Aqua* is Latin for "water".

Wood for making scaffolding

Were they easy to build?

No. They are examples of very clever Roman building and design. Water cannot flow uphill, so it was very important that an aqueduct was built at exactly the right angle. Otherwise the water might flow back to where it came from! Most aqueducts were over 17m (55ft) high. One famous aqueduct stretched for over 55km (34miles).

30

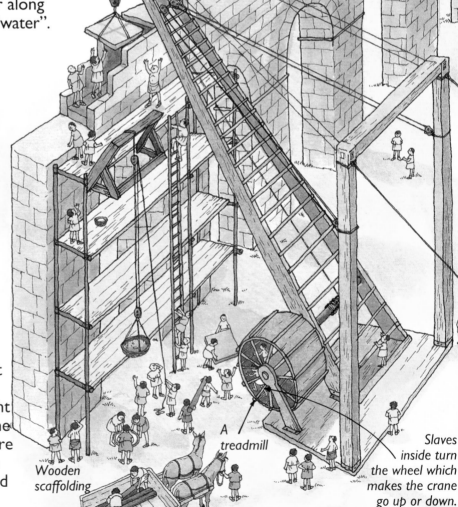

Wooden scaffolding

A treadmill

Slaves inside turn the wheel which makes the crane go up or down.

Road

These workers are slaves.

These soldiers are working on the road.

Two tired mules

Why are Roman roads so famous?

Partly because many modern roads follow the path of old Roman roads, partly because Roman roads were so straight, and partly because they were so well made.

How was a Roman road made?

To start with, the shortest, flattest route was chosen. Then the area was cleared of trees and rocks. After that, a 1m (3ft) trench was dug and filled with stones of different sizes. The top layer of stones had a mound in the middle. This was so that rainwater would run down the sides into ditches.

This is a typical Roman road.   *Lump in middle called a camber*   *Ditch for rainwater*

Small stones, sometimes mixed with cement   *Tightly-packed gravel*   *Bottom layer of large stones*

Why were they built so high up?

Not only to control the flow of water. It also made it difficult for people to steal the water, and much harder for enemies to put poison in it.

Did you know?

The Latin for "lead" is *plumbum*, which is where the word "plumbing" comes from. When the water from an aqueduct reached a city, it was fed into lead pipes under the ground. How many different uses for water can you remember from this book?

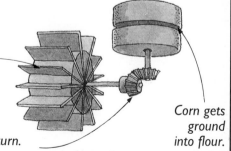

A water wheel

Water flows through here.

Wheel turns

Turning wheel makes stones turn.

Corn gets ground into flour.

Index

Answers

Page 8.
To make it hotter, they probably made a bigger fire.
Page 13.
The number 4 on a clock is often shown as IIII instead of IV.
Page 15.
It is a set of false teeth.
Page 19.
They made copies of Roman instruments and played them!
Page 26.
They are Minerva, Bacchus and Mercury.
Page 31.
There are lots of different uses for water, from cooking to bathing. You'll have to look back through the book to find them!

First published in 1993 by Usborne Publishing Ltd, Usborne House 83-85 Saffron Hill, London EC1N 8RT, England. Copyright © Usborne Publishing Ltd.

The name Usborne and the device are Trade Marks of Usborne Publishing Ltd. All rights reserved.

First published in America March 1994
Printed in Belgium.
UE